Top Piano Hits FOR DUMMIES®

Performance Notes by
Adam Perlmutter

D1452297

ISBN: 978-1-4803-4505-8

CORPORATION

7777 W. BLUEMOUND RD. P.O. BOX 13819 MILWAUKEE, WI 53213

Visit Hal Leonard Online at
www.halleonard.com

MAR 2 3 2015

Table of Contents

· ·

Introduction

Welcome to *Top Piano Hits For Dummies*. In this book you'll find arrangements of 36 popular piano-driven songs in a range of musical idioms — everything from empowering ballads like Christina Aguilera's "Beautiful," to modern country chart-toppers like "Wanted" by Hunter Hayes, to more experimental rock fare such as Radiohead's "Pyramid Song." The music notation includes a self-contained piano arrangement as well as a vocal line with lyrics, plus guitar-chord frames for each song. Also included are performance notes that provide background for the artists and their tunes, as well as tips like technical suggestions and musical analysis — in other words, everything you need to make these great songs your own. Enjoy!

About This Book

For each song, I include a bit of background information to satisfy the historically curious. The information is followed by a variety of tidbits that struck me as I made my way through the teaching of these songs, including some of the following:

- A run-down of the parts you need to know.

- A breakdown of some of the chord progressions you need to navigate the sheet music.

- Some tips and shortcuts you can use to expedite the learning process.

In many cases, you may already know how to do a lot of this. If so, feel free to skip over those familiar bits.

How to Use This Book

The music contains vocal and piano parts and guitar frames for each song. And included throughout are handy performance notes to help you learn how to play these songs and understand how they work. I recommend that you first play through the song, and then practice all the main sections and chords. From there, you can add the tricks and treats of each one — and there are many. Approach each song one section at a time and then assemble the sections together in a sequence. This technique helps to provide you with a greater understanding of how the song is structured, and enables you to play it through more quickly.

In order to follow the music and my performance notes, you need a basic understanding of scales and chords. But if you're not a wiz, don't worry. Just spend a little time with the nifty tome *Music Theory For Dummies* by Michael Pilhofer and Holly Day (Wiley), and with a little practice, you'll be on your way to entertaining family and friends.

Conventions Used in This Book

As you might expect, I use quite a few musical terms in this book. Some of these may be unfamiliar to you, so here are a few right off the bat that can help your understanding of basic playing principles:

✔ **Arpeggio:** Playing the notes of a chord one at a time rather than all together.

✔ **Bridge:** Part of the song that is different from the verse and the chorus, providing variety and connecting the other parts of the song to each other.

✔ **Coda:** The section at the end of the song, which is sometimes labeled with the word "coda."

✔ **Chorus:** The part of the song that is the same each time through, usually the most familiar section.

✔ **Hook:** A familiar, accessible, or sing-along melody, lick, or other section of the song.

✔ **Verse:** The part of the song that tells the story; each verse has different lyrics, and each song generally has between two and four of these.

Icons Used in This Book

In the margins of this book are several handy icons to help make following the performance notes easier:

These are optional parts, or alternate approaches that those who'd like to find their way through the song with a distinctive flair can take. Often these are slightly more challenging routes, but encouraged nonetheless, because there's nothing like a good challenge!

This is where you will find notes about specific musical concepts that are relevant but confusing to non-musical types — stuff that you wouldn't bring up, say, at a frat party or at your kid's soccer game.

You get lots of these tips, because the more playing suggestions I can offer, the better you'll play. And isn't that what it's all about?

The A Team

Words and Music by Ed Sheeran

Apologize

Words and Music by Ryan Tedder

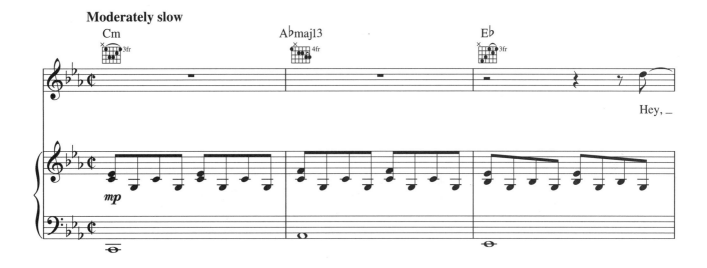

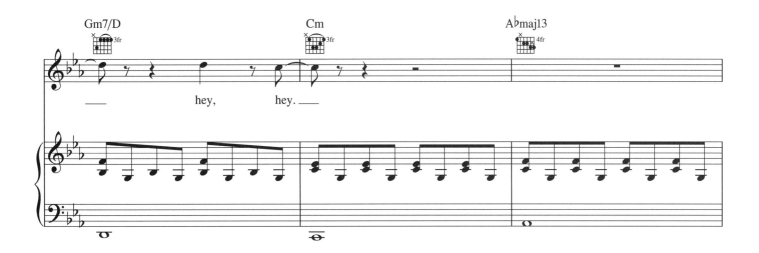

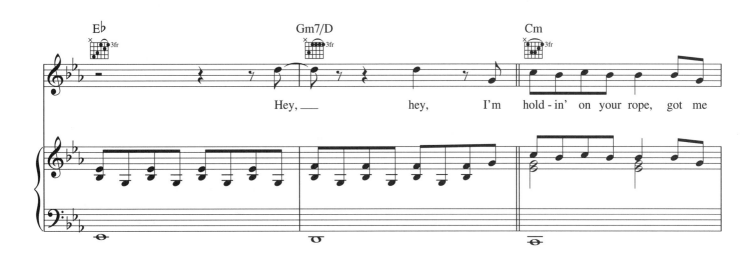

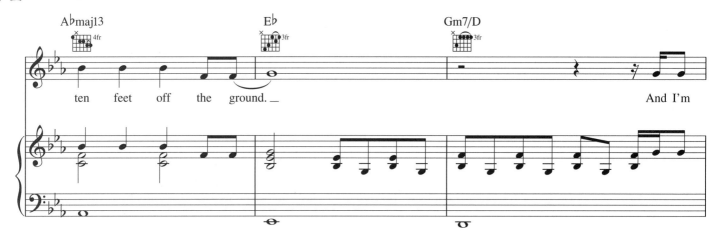

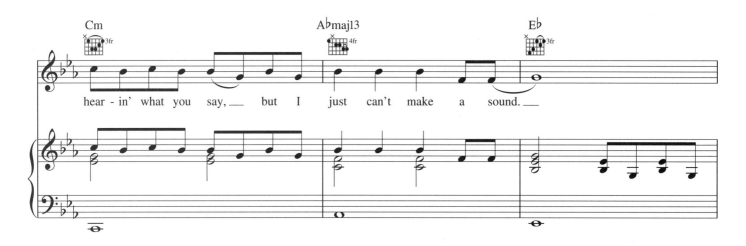

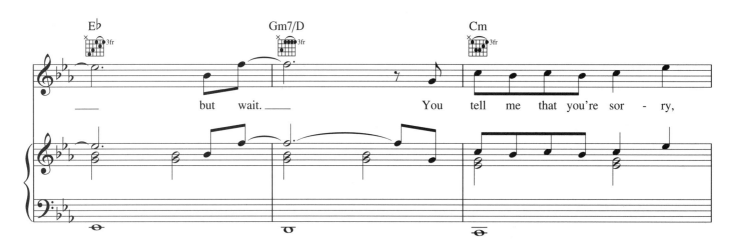

Bad Day

Words and Music by Daniel Powter

Beautiful

Words and Music by Linda Perry

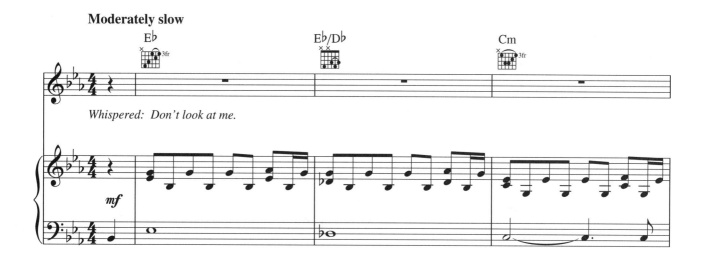

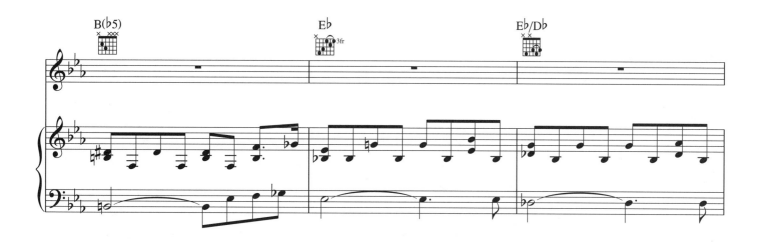

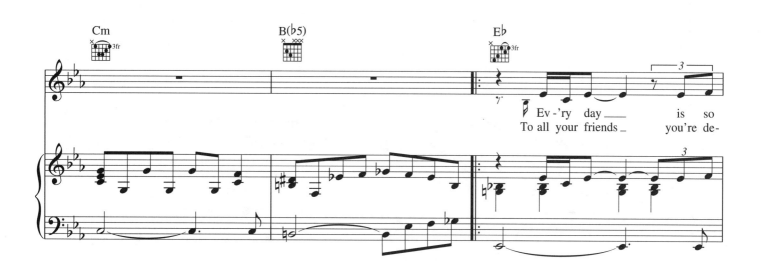

Because of You

Words and Music by Kelly Clarkson, David Hodges and Ben Moody

Recorded a half step higher.

Brave

Words and Music by Sara Bareilles and Jack Antonoff

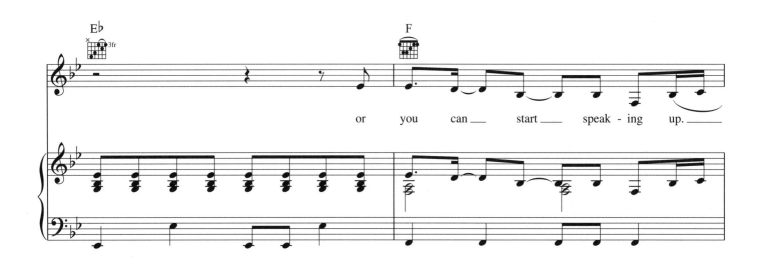

I wan-na see you be brave. ___ Ev-'ry-bod-y's been there, ev-'ry-bod-y's

been stared ___ down by the en-e-my. ___ Fall-en for the fear and done some dis-ap-

pear-in', bow down to the might-y. Don't ___ run, just stop hold-in' your tongue.

May-be there's a way out of the cage where you live. May-be one of these

Call Me Maybe

Words and Music by Carly Rae Jepsen, Joshua Ramsay and Tavish Crowe

Moderate Pop

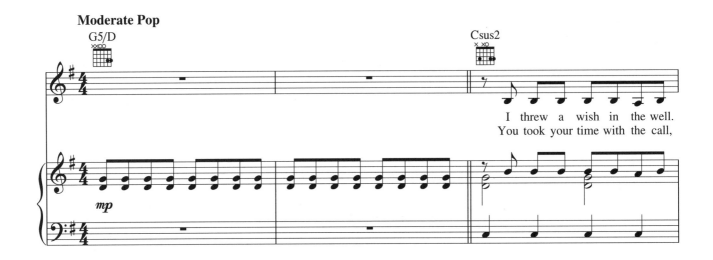

I threw a wish in the well.
You took your time with the call,

Don't ask me, I'll nev-er tell.
I took no time with the fall.

I looked to you as it fell
You gave me noth-in' at all,

and now you're in my ___ way.
but still you're in my ___ way.

I trade my soul for a wish,
I beg and bor-row and steal,

pen-nies and dimes for a kiss.
at first sight and it's real.

I was-n't look-in' for this,
I did-n't know I would feel

Colorblind

Words by Adam F. Duritz
Music by Adam F. Duritz and Charles Gillingham

Fireflies

Words and Music by Adam Young

Girl on Fire

Words and Music by Alicia Keys, Salaam Remi, Jeff Bhasker, Nicki Minaj and Billy Squier

Halo

Words and Music by Beyoncé Knowles, Ryan Tedder and Evan Bogart

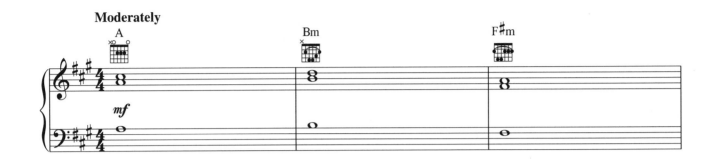

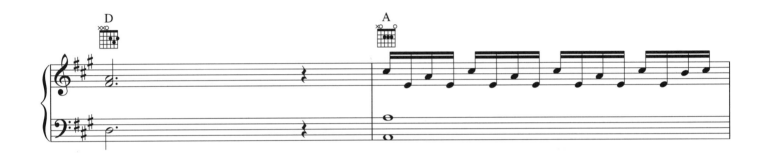

Re-mem-ber those walls I built?

*Verse one is written an octave higher than sung.

*Lead vocal sung both times at written pitch.

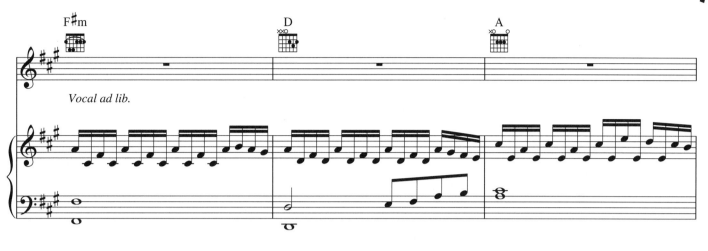

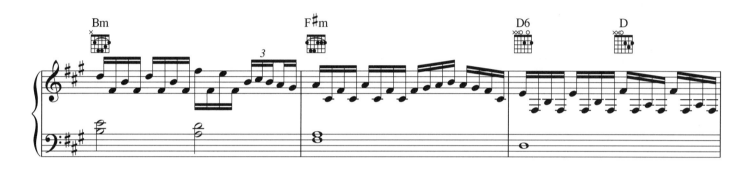

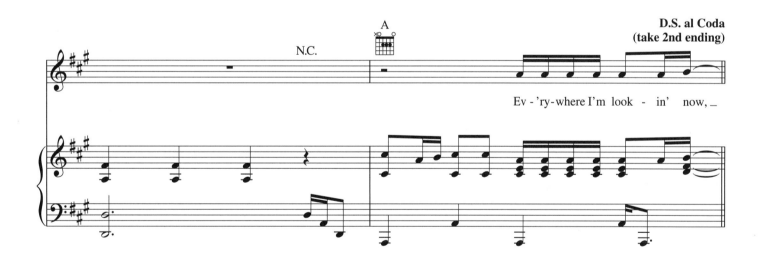

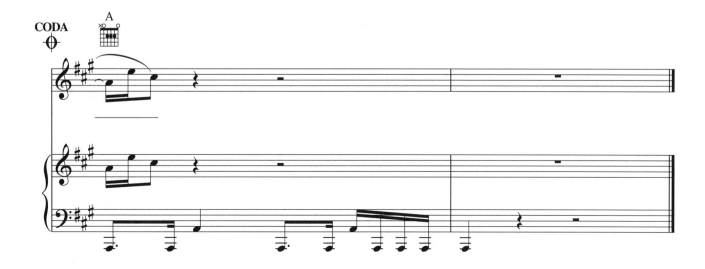

Home

Words and Music by Amy Foster-Gillies, Michael Bublé and Alan Chang

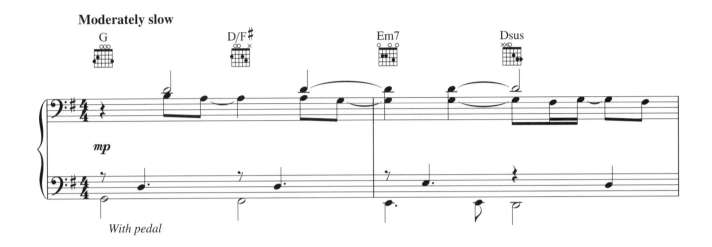

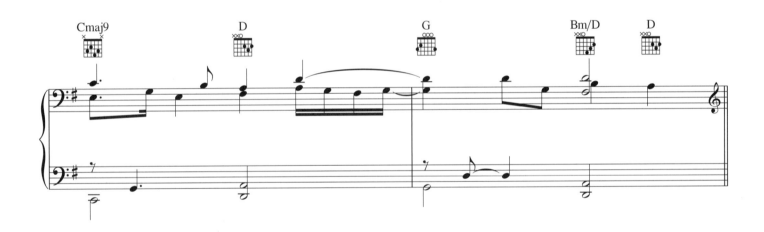

An oth-er sum-mer day   has come and gone a-way   in Par-is and Rome, _   but I wan-na go home. _

Home

Words and Music by Greg Holden and Drew Pearson

lost, you __ can al - ways __ be found. Just

know you're not a - lone, _____

'cause I'm gon - na make this place your _____ home.

How to Save a Life

Words and Music by Joseph King and Isaac Slade

I Knew You Were Trouble.

Words and Music by Taylor Swift, Shellback and Max Martin

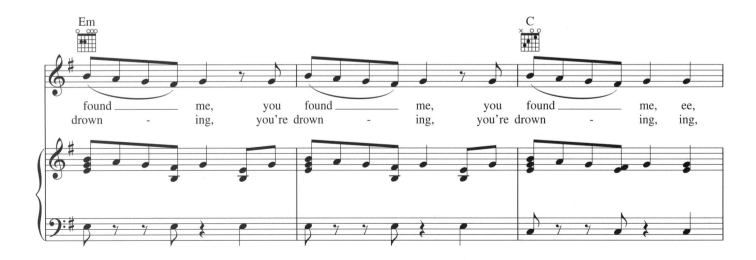

ee,   ee,   ee.   I guess you did-n't care   and I guess I liked that.   And
ing,   ing,   ing. And I heard you moved_ on   from_ whis-pers on the street.   A

when I fell   hard,   you took a step_ back   with - out _____ me,   with -
new notch in your belt   is all I'll ev - er be.   And now _____ I see,

out _____ me,   with - out _____ me,   ee,   ee,   ee,   ee. _____
now _____ I see,   now _____ I see, ee,   ee,   ee,   ee. _____

And he's long _____ gone   when he's next_
He was long _____ gone   when he met_

It's Time

Words and Music by Daniel Reynolds, Benjamin McKee and Daniel Sermon

Now, don't you un - der - stand _____ that I'm

nev - er chang - ing who I am?

Jar of Hearts

Words and Music by Barrett Yeretsian, Christina Perri and Drew Lawrence

Moderate Ballad

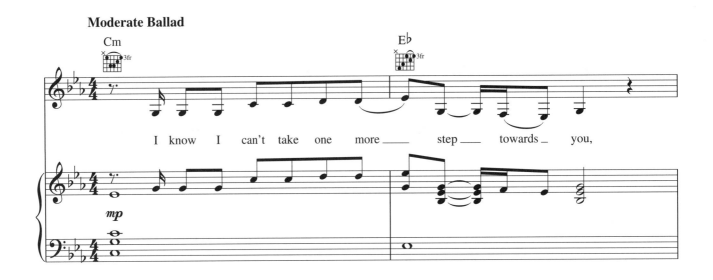

get me back. _____ And who do you think you are, _

run-ning 'round leav - ing scars, _____ col - lect - ing your jar of hearts _

and tear - ing love a - part? _____ You're gon - na catch __ a cold __

from the ice in - side __ your soul. _____ So don't come back for

me,   don't come back   at   all.

Who   do   you   think   you _____ are?

Who   do   you   think   you _____ are?

Who   do   you   think   you   are?

rit.

Just Give Me a Reason

Words and Music by Alecia Moore, Jeff Bhasker and Nate Ruess

Performance Notes

The A Team *(page 6)*

In his early 20s at the time of this writing, the English singer-songwriter and Atlantic recording artist Ed Sheeran already had a string of hits under his belt. Among Sheeran's strongest songs is his 2011 debut single, "The A Team," which he penned in his university flat and recorded for under £200. The tune's dark subject matter, the deleterious effects of drugs, was inspired by a girl named Angel, who Sheeran met while volunteering in a homeless shelter. "The A Team" was an immediate hit, selling 200,000 copies within a couple weeks of its release, and it went on to debut at #5 on Billboard's 200 and #1 on the Folk Albums chart — a staggering success for a newcomer.

"The A Team" is melodically and harmonically straightforward, but rhythmically complex because of its extensive syncopation. If the rhythms look challenging to you, focus on them before tackling the piece on the piano. Instead of feeling the music in quarter notes, try 16ths, counting, "One-ee-and-uh, two-ee-and-uh, three-ee-and-uh, four-ee-and-uh," and so on. So, in the right hand (upper bass clef) of the first measure, the notes fall on the "and" of beat 1, the "ee" of beat 2, the "and" of beat 3, and the "ee" of beat 4. Focusing on the rhythm in this way (called *subdividing*) helps ensure that you learn the entire tune more efficiently.

Apologize *(page 11)*

OneRepublic, a pop-rock band from Colorado Springs, Colorado, achieved astonishing success while unsigned, thanks to the power of the Internet, specifically the website MySpace. The group's first single, "Apologize" (2007), earned the distinction of becoming the most played single in the history of American radio, heard 10,394 times in one week. The song went on to be an international hit and made its way to #10 on Billboard's Hot 100 Songs of the Decade. But what is perhaps most surprising about the tune is that the rapper Timbaland appropriated it on his album *Shock Value*, a testament to the song's great durability.

Played in the brooding key of C minor, "Apologize" is largely *triadic*, which means it contains mostly three-note chords. But the song does have some spots that imply more complex harmonies, such as an A♭maj13 chord, which is an A♭maj7 chord (A♭–C–E♭–G) that also includes the 13th degree (F), and a Gm7/D chord, which can be thought of as a G minor triad with an added seventh (G–B♭–D–F) with the fifth, D, in the bass. When playing through the song, take the time to get the sounds of these chords in your head and enjoy the subtle sophistication they bring to the music.

Bad Day (page 18)

Few songs of the 2000s were as hot as the Canadian singer-songwriter Daniel Powter's "Bad Day," which was heard in a 2005 European Coca-Cola commercial before becoming the most successful single of 2006. The song was so popular as to figure prominently in the fifth season of American Idol. But Powter has been unable to pen another song so universally loved; in 2009, in fact, *Billboard* named him as the decade's one-hit wonder. Still, "Bad Day" continues to remind listeners to see the big picture on those occasions when things just aren't going their way.

"Bad Day" is written in the key of E♭ major, and the song's rhythmic notation is perhaps its most tricky aspect. The song contains plenty of syncopated 16th-note rhythms, so take learning the song at a glacial pace, subdividing if needed. Also be aware of the song's "feel" at the 16th-note level as opposed to the more common eighth-note level. Note the indication at the tempo head, "Moderate groove." Wherever you see a pair of consecutive 16ths, play and sing the first note for longer than the second (at roughly a 2:1 ratio between the two notes). Sound confusing? Then simply listen closely to Daniel Powter's original recording of the song before playing along with it.

Beautiful (page 25)

Along with Justin Timberlake and Britney Spears, Christina Aguilera used a youthful appearance on television's *The Mickey Mouse Club* as a springboard for a career as a mega-successful singer-songwriter. Aguilera's strongest song is the 2002 ballad "Beautiful," which was written by Linda Perry of 4 Non Blondes. The song, which chronicles the struggles of a woman who has overcome feelings of insecurity, proved universally empowering. It was listed at #52 on *Rolling Stone*'s Top 100 songs of the 2000s and has been covered by artists as unlikely as Elvis Costello, who recorded an interpretation for an episode of the TV show *House M.D.*, and the indie-rock bands Clem Snide and The Lemonheads.

"Beautiful" is fairly easy to learn, but it offers a few challenges. The song starts with a *pickup measure* that has fewer beats than a full bar of the given meter. In this case, the first note falls squarely on beat 4. Beginning in the ninth full bar, you see cue-size (miniaturized) notes; these are to be ignored the first time through and sung on the repeat. In the last measure of the song, you see fermata signs ⌢, which call for you to hold the notes for an unspecified duration, as long as you'd like. Let the music hang in the air for dramatic effect here.

Because of You (page 30)

Kelly Clarkson is among a handful of singers to have emerged as stars after being winning contestants on the television show *American Idol*. One of Clarkson's most popular songs is "Because of You," which she originally wrote as a teenager in response to the intense emotions she felt during her parents' divorce. Clarkson had intended to include the song on her 2003 debut, *Thankful*, but her record label didn't agree. Luckily, though, a retooled version of the song made it to her sophomore effort, *Breakaway* (2004). The single, which peaked at #7 on Billboard's Hot 100 and has sold over 1.5 million digital downloads, clearly resonated with fans the world over.

Though it was originally recorded in the key of F minor, "Because of You" is arranged here a half step lower, in the easier key of E minor. Heads-up on some areas that might trip you up: At bar 12, the music changes to 2/4 meter from 4/4, then back again in the next measure. Be careful to maintain a steady rhythm during this transition; if necessary use a metronome. Later in the song the music modulates up a whole step, to the key of F# minor, and it's important to transition smoothly here, so isolate this area and practice it slowly if needed. Also, be sure to observe the emotional lift created by this modulation.

Brave (page 36)

The lead single from her 2013 CD *Blessed Unrest*, Sara Bareilles' "Brave" is a rhythmically upbeat, fast-paced pop tune with a positive message. The song debuted at #61 on the Billboard Hot 100. Bareilles said its universal "believe in yourself" message was inspired by a close friend struggling with an important decision.

Notice the driving rhythmic pattern in the left hand of the piano accompaniment. Although the notes change from measure to measure, the rhythm stays the same through the entire verse. Don't let the sixteenth notes in the right-hand part slow you down. Just sing along with the lyrics, and the bouncy vibe of this song will carry you along.

Call Me Maybe (page 42)

Not only did the Canadian singer-songwriter Carly Rae Jepson's 2011 song "Call Me Maybe" inspire a raft of viral tributes, the phrase "call me maybe" has made its way into the vernacular of dating. Whether or not this tactic is clever or corny is debatable, but what is certain is that the infectious tune, which started life as a folk song and was released as a dance track, is a pop-culture phenomenon. Internationally popular, the song peaked at #2 on *Billboard*'s Hot 100 and has sold more than seven million copies in the U.S. alone.

The right-hand part of "Call Me Maybe" is divided into two layers: the up-stemmed notes double the vocal melody and the down-stemmed ones provide harmonic support. If you have difficulty playing the music as written, break things down by learning the top layer and bottom layer separately before merging them. Then, learn the bass part on its own and, finally, combine everything. This song makes a very basic chord progression a little more interesting with the use of sus2 chords (Csus2 and Dsus2). Sus2 chords are triads in which the third is replaced with the second. Be sure to compare these chords to their major counterparts (for example, C–D–G and C–E–G) to appreciate the difference this simple modification makes.

Colorblind (page 46)

Hailing from Berkeley, California, the alternative rock band Counting Crows became an overnight sensation with the release of their debut album, *August and Everything After*, featuring the hit single "Mr. Jones," in 1993. Like a number of songs in this collection, Counting Crows' "Colorblind" sounds as if it were made for the screen. And it has, in fact, been heard on an episode of *Roswell* and in the film *Cruel Intentions*. The tune was featured on the band's third studio album, *This Desert Life* (1999). Our arrangement for voice and piano translates well to your practice or living room.

Though the first chord of the main progression, Am7, might suggest that "Colorblind" is in the key of A minor, it is actually in the key of F major. This is due to extensive use of the F chord and the fact that the piece ends on an F triad, to say nothing of the B♭s in the melody. The use of the Am7 chord in this context gives the music a hauntingly ambiguous quality. Contributing to this is the looseness of the tempo. Whenever you see the indication *rit. (ritardando)*, slow down, and where you see *a tempo*, return to the previous tempo. Throughout, strive for a lyrical quality, and let the piano arpeggios ring together flowingly.

Fireflies (page 52)

Owl City is an electronica project from the singer-songwriter Adam Young, a Minnesota native whose earliest songs were recorded in his parents' basement. Much of Young's music has an ethereal, atmospheric sound, which he thinks was originally sparked by a reaction against the dreariness of working in a Coca-Cola warehouse as a day job. One of the best examples of Young's works is his song "Fireflies," a worldwide success in 2009 and 2010, which peaked at #1 on *Billboard*'s U.S. Hot 100, and was even heard in the video games Guitar Hero 5 and Rock Band 3.

Pop music often makes the most from a minimum of materials, as is seen in "Fireflies," notated here in the key of E♭ major. Scan through the music and you'll see that most of the song is built on the most basic chords: I, IV, and V (E♭, A♭, and B♭). Essentially, this means that once you've polished off the first two bars of the verse, you'll know the bulk of the song. So, take your time in learning that portion, slowing things down and subdividing in order to really nail those syncopated 16th notes.

Girl on Fire (page 59)

Few contemporary R&B singer-songwriters are as figuratively on fire as Alicia Keys, who has sold over 35 million albums and 30 singles worldwide, sweeping up a number of awards in the process. The lead single from Keys' fifth studio album, "Girl on Fire" (2012) is a mid-tempo number inspired by her marriage and the birth of a son. It peaked at #2 on *Billboard*'s Hot R&B/Hip-Hop Songs chart and was a smash hit around the world as well. For the album, Keys recorded a three-track suite of "Girl on Fire," and our piano-vocal-guitar arrangement is based on the main version.

"Girl on Fire" appears in the key of A major. Like all other R&B and gospel vocalists, Keys sings a lot of *melismatic* phrases, those in which a single syllable is assigned to a string of notes. In notation, such a phrase is indicated by a curved line connecting the first and last notes, with a corresponding horizontal line extending the duration of the phrase in the lyrics. To learn the song, first isolate all the melismatic passages, making sure that you have them down cold in terms of intonation and evenness before tackling the entire song. Then, when you put everything together, be sure to take an ample breath just before the start of each phrase.

Halo (page 66)

A contemporary of Alicia Keys, Beyoncé Knowles (best known by her stage name, Beyoncé) is another young queen of R&B. Beyoncé first ascended to fame in the late 1990s as a member of Destiny's Child, one of the most popular girl groups of all time. In 2003 she stepped out on her own with the debut album *Dangerously in Love*. She has since sold over 13 million albums in the U.S. and 118 million worldwide, making her one of the best-selling musical artists of any persuasion. From Beyoncé's third studio album, *I Am... Sasha Fierce* (2008), "Halo," was a chart-topping single around the world. The song gives listeners a glimpse into the artist's private life.

"Halo" is arranged here in the key of A major. Like many songs in this collection, it features a road map that isn't as complicated as it looks. But in the event you find yourself confused, here's exactly how to proceed:

1. **Play the music from the beginning until the repeat sign.**
2. **Go back to play the second verse, and play the second ending.**
3. **Continue after the second ending, until you reach the instruction D.S. al Coda (take 2nd ending).**
4. **Go back to the coda sign next to the Bm guitar frame.**
5. **Follow the music, skipping the first ending and taking the second ending, until you reach the measure marked To Coda.**
6. **Jump ahead to the coda to play the final two bars of the song.**

Home (Michael Bublé) (page 72)

Not to be confused with the following selection, this "Home" was a breakthrough for the Canadian singer-songwriter Michael Bublé. The 2005 song dealt with Bublé's sadness in being on the road and apart from his then-wife-to-be. It received a relatively low-profile release but quickly peaked at #1 on *Billboard*'s Adult Contemporary chart. It made its way onto the big screen, in *The Wedding Date*, and also became a hit for the country crooner Blake Shelton. Just as Shelton and Bublé have been known to sing the song together on occasion, you can play it with your friends with our piano/vocal arrangement.

Both hands are in the bass clef until the sign on page two, when the right hand moves back to its customary treble clef. In the measure before that change, on beat 2, note that the 16th-note run starts on the left hand but transfers to the right; make sure to articulate this detail smoothly, with equal volume between hands. Heads-up, too, on the quick change from 4/4 to 2/4 and back on the third page of the music, and for the bit of *contrary motion* (two voices moving in an opposite direction) on the second bar at the top of the fifth page.

Home (*Phillip Phillips*) (*page 78*)

"Home" is one of the most popular pieces of original music ever featured on the television show *American Idol*. The winner of season 11, Phillip Phillips, first performed the song on the final performance night, in May, 2012, and he later recorded it as his debut single. "Home" was a smash hit, peaking at #1 on both the Adult Pop Songs and Adult Contemporary charts and at #2 on the Rock Songs chart. On the original recording, the song is driven by a traditionally fingerpicked acoustic guitar, but it lends itself nicely to the piano, as in our arrangement.

Play "Home" brightly and with a feeling of two beats per measure — think of a traditional bluegrass or country feel. This time signature, also known as *cut time*, is indicated at the beginning of the song by the C with a vertical line through it. Feel it by counting in half notes, two per bar, rather than quarter notes. To further enhance the down-homey feel, when you play the piano part, imagine that your left hand is a string bass and your right a banjo or guitar. Also, as indicated at the beginning of the song, use the pedal, but do so judiciously, so that the notes don't all turn to mush.

How to Save a Life (*page 85*)

The piano-driven rock band The Fray came together in 2002 when classmates Isaac Slade and Joe King formed a band in Denver, Colorado. Within several years the group had a certified double-platinum album in its 2005 debut, *How to Save a Life*. The title track, which was inspired by Slade's experiences working at a camp for troubled youths, is the Fray's most popular song to date. It topped the Adult Top 50 chart for 15 weeks in a row and sold nearly four million downloads. Plus it appeared in television's *Grey's Anatomy* and *Scrubs*, among other shows. Prominent elements of the song's infectious piano part are preserved here in our piano-vocal-guitar arrangement.

The music in the first four bars of "How to Save a Life" provides a pattern for the entire song, so focus on this introductory section before continuing. In the left hand, consider learning the up-stemmed eighth notes before adding the whole notes underneath. Also be aware of the song's use of dynamics. The verses should be played and sung *mezzo-piano* (*mp*), moderately quiet, while the chorus sections are *mezzo-forte* (*mf*), moderately loud. It's important to have varied dynamics in music, for if you always played at the same volume level you sound monotonous.

I Knew You Were Trouble. (*page 92*)

"I Knew You Were Trouble.," by the country-pop singer-songwriter Taylor Swift, is a song about reprimanding oneself on a poor choice of romantic partner. The song is both mainstream and experimental bearing the influence of *dubstep*, an electronic dance cousin of reggae that emerged in South London. Selling a whopping 416,000 copies in its first week, the song hit *Billboard*'s Hot 100 chart at #3 and ascended to #1, where it stayed for four weeks. Our arrangement will have you creating some cool dubstep moves at the piano.

With "I Knew You Were Trouble." Taylor Swift uses one of the most common chord progressions, I–V–vi–IV (G–D–Em–C), to create music that's all her own. Although it might look easy, achieving the dubstep feel requires that you play with great rhythmic precision. Focus on the rhythm of the bass line in particular. When learning this part, count "*One*-and, two-*and*, three-and, *four*-and," with a note falling on each accented syllable. Make sure you don't let the first and second notes of each bar fall beyond their designated value of an eighth note: As with so many other idioms, reggae and dubstep rely as much on the beats that aren't played as the ones that are.

It's Time (page 98)

An indie-rock band from Las Vegas, Imagine Dragons was formed in 2008 in Utah by the singer Dan Reynolds and the guitarist Wayne Sermon. The band recorded three EPs on its own before releasing a breakthrough EP, *Continued Silence*, on Interscope Records, in 2012. The rollicking single "It's Time" reached #15 on *Billboard*'s Hot 100, and the band made the rounds of all the late-night talk shows playing the song. Our arrangement distills this spirited tune, filled with old-time instruments and handclaps, into a handy piano-vocal-guitar arrangement.

"It's Time" only has five chords: D, Asus4, Bm, G, and E, which are reordered in such a way that they create changes in mood during different sections of the song. The opening four bars are an arrangement of the mandolin part heard on the original recording, so if you have someone who can play mandolin, banjo, or guitar at your disposal feel free to add this part to the verse. While you're at it, to complete the Appalachian-inspired atmosphere, have someone with free hands add a recurring "*One*-two-*three*-four-one-two" handclap to the proceedings.

Jar of Hearts (page 106)

The debut single of the American singer-songwriter Christina Perri, "Jar of Hearts" was first heard on the televised competition *So You Think You Can Dance*, before Perri had even signed a record deal. Released on iTunes in 2010, the apparently autobiographical number (in which an ex tries to reignite a failed relationship), proved instantly popular, spending 23 weeks on *Billboard*'s Hot 100 and peaking at #17. This piano-driven ballad lends itself perfectly to our arrangement for vocals and piano with suggested chord frames for guitar.

"Jar of Hearts" is written in the key of C minor. If you scan the notation you'll see that certain chord symbols contain two letters. These are called *slash* chords. No, they're not named after the top-hat-wearing guitarist from the rock band Guns N' Roses. Instead, the symbol to the left of the slash indicates the chord to be played, and that to the right depicts the bass note, which is a note other than the root of the chord. In this song, slash chords are used to create smoothly connected bass lines and add harmonic flavor. For instance, in the progression Cm–G/B–E♭/B♭–F7/A–A♭ the slash chords allow the bass line to move straight down the C minor scale.

Just Give Me a Reason (page 114)

"Just Give Me a Reason" is a single by the American pop star Pink in collaboration with the band fun.'s lead singer, Nate Ruess. The song's subject matter happens to be not so fun: desperately clinging to a relationship as it is falling apart. It was an international smash hit, peaking at #1 in countries from Australia to Slovakia. Another piano-driven song, "Just Give Me a Reason" has good reason to be included in this collection of piano-centered arrangements.

"Just Give Me a Reason" is for the most part straightforward, but has a couple of potentially tricky rhythms. Midway through the song is a *quarter-note triplet* (three quarter notes in the space usually taken up by two), indicated with a bracketed 3. To feel this rhythm, try counting eighth note triplets on each beat: "trip-uh-let, trip-uh-let," and so on. In the span of two beats, quarter notes will fall on the first "trip," the first "let," and the second "uh." Near the end of the song is a 16th-note sextuplet, or six notes in the space of one quarter note. If you have a problem negotiating this rhythm, subdivide and think of it as two 16th-note triplets.

Love Song (page 136)

"Love Song" is the debut single of the American singer-songwriter-pianist Sara Bareilles. The 2007 song, which Bareilles says wrote itself, remained on the *Billboard* Hot 100 for 41 weeks, peaking at #1. It also made its way into the American TV show *Glee* and the Brazilian soap opera *Beleza Pura*, and has even received a punk treatment, courtesy of the band Four Year Strong. Six years after its release, "Love Song" remains Bareilles' strongest song, with its swinging rhythms and catchy hooks.

Key to playing "Love Song" is nailing its rhythmic feel. As indicated at the top of the notation, the music is to be played with a swing feel; a pair of consecutive eighth notes should be rendered not equally as written but long-short, at roughly a two-to-one ratio. The song's basic rhythm includes a chord stab played on each downbeat, four per measure; be sure to cut these chords short as shown by the eighth notes in the notation. When playing the bass part, remember that the notes on the "ands" of certain beats are delayed slightly while the rests that precede them are held longer than usual. If the swing feel eludes you, simply play along with the original recording, and if needed, use computer software to slow down the recording to a manageable tempo as you play.

The Luckiest (page 150)

Not many musicians do piano rock as skillfully and tastefully as Ben Folds, the singer-songwriter-instrumentalist and leader of Ben Folds Five. The ensemble rose to fame in the early 1990s, disbanding in 2000 only to officially regroup a dozen years later. "The Luckiest" comes from Folds' 2001 solo album, *Rockin' the Suburbs*. Although this song wasn't as popular as the title track, which peaked at #28 on *Billboard*'s Modern Rock Tracks chart, it is nonetheless a beautiful song and a pleasure to play on the piano.

"The Luckiest" is shown here in the easy key of D major, with no accidentals to be seen, but its reliance on 16th-note syncopations can make it difficult for some. If you have trouble, learn each hand independently, and subdivide, paying close attention to the placement of the notes and the rests. After you put everything together, strive for a flowing, lyrical feel, adding pedal if you wish, and wherever you see the indication *poco rit.* slow down slightly, returning to the original tempo as directed. One other thing: In the terminal bar, the indication *8va bassa* simply calls for the note to be played an octave lower than written.

My Immortal (page 145)

A piano rock song, "My Immortal" comes from the band Evanescence's 2003 debut album, *Fallen*. The tune dates back to a 1997 demo that singer Amy Lee made at the age of 16. With Evanescence's signature moody sound, the song charted well around the world, hitting #1 in the U.S., Canada, Greece, and the UK. In 2005 it was nominated for a GRAMMY® for Best Pop Performance by a Duo or Group with Vocals, and it has remained the group's most successful song to date.

"My Immortal" has a simple progression that toggles between the A and C#m chords. In much of the song, the stark arrangement captures the moody quality of the original recording, while harmonies are implied by the melody and bass notes. In the introduction the chords are spelled out with piano arpeggios. In the first four bars, the only note that changes between the two chords is the root note (A) of the A chord, which moves down a half step to a G#, the fifth of the C# minor chord. This is known as *voice leading*, which makes for the smoothest transition between the chords.

Next to Me (page 154)

"Next to Me" is Scottish singer-songwriter Emeli Sandé's 2012 international hit. Released in February, the song debuted at #1 on the Irish Singles Chart, topped the Scottish Singles Chart, and hit #2 on the UK Singles Chart. An April release in the U.S. saw "Next to Me' climb to #25 on the Billboard Hot 100.

As you play this rhythmic anthem, lean into the driving bass progression and enjoy the gospel harmony. The moving eighth notes will help you feel the syncopation in the melody line. If you find yourself struggling with the sixteenth note-eighth note-sixteenth note rhythm that is the backbone of this song, play that melody line with the right hand as you tap or play even eighths in your left hand. Start slowly, add the lyrics, and soon you'll find your groove!

Pyramid Song (page 158)

Few rock bands are both as wildly successful and as boldly experimental as Radiohead. The band's music owes as much to the French composer Olivier Messiaen as it does to alternative rock groups like Sonic Youth and jazz luminaries like Charles Mingus. "Pyramid Song" is the first single from Radiohead's 2001 album *Amnesiac*, and ranked among Rolling Stone's 100 Best Songs of the Decade.

Before you dive into the music, note that "Pyramid Song" kicks off on an exotic chord progression: F#-Gmaj7-A6, which gives it a haunting sound. Take a moment to enjoy these sonorities and the mood they impart. Also note how the progression rises and falls. This will add expressiveness to your performance.

The Scientist (page 162)

Another great band from across the pond, Coldplay achieved worldwide fame with the 2000 debut *Parachutes* (featuring the single "Yellow"), then managed to avoid the sophomore slump with its second album, *A Rush of Blood to the Head* (2001). "The Scientist" was included in that album, in NME's "150 Best Tracks of the Past 15 Years" in 2011, and has been covered by artists ranging from Willie Nelson to the cast of television's *Glee*. A curious detail: the word "scientist" doesn't make an appearance in the lyrics to this yearning song, which isn't about a researcher, but about the prospect of a romantic reconciliation.

"The Scientist" is built from some pretty rudimentary rhythms, with unshakably steady eighth notes in the bass. So, instead of busying yourself with negotiating the rhythms, you can relax and focus on the song's attractive harmonic work. Look at the music and you'll see that it kicks off on a Dm7 chord (D-F-A-C), which adds a wistful quality that complements the lyrics. For comparison, relieve the chord of its seventh (C), to witness what expressive power this single note has. Similarly, take the Fsus2 chord (F-G-C), resolve its second degree, G, up to the third, to A, and the music will sound a bit plainer. Subtle details like these can really make the difference between a captivating song and a pedestrian one.

Skyfall (page 176)

From the 2012 James Bond film of the same name, "Skyfall" was written and performed by the English singer-songwriter Adele. As befits the big screen, the song is a hyperballad, in which the vocals and piano accompaniment are supported by a soaring orchestral score. It was extremely well received, winning the Academy Award for Best Original Song and the Brit Award for Best British Single, among a handful of other accolades. You can harness the power of this very moving theme in our special arrangement.

Before you delve into "Skyfall," in the key of C minor, check out the first chord, Cm(add9), which is a C minor triad (C-E♭-G) topped with the ninth (D). This big-sounding sonority makes an appearance throughout the *James Bond* series of films. Also make sure that you know how to count all the rhythms in the piece before you even touch the piano. If you find yourself struggling rhythmically, slow things down and subdivide, counting in 16th notes instead of quarters. The measures that have 32nd notes will be the trickiest. Practice slowly until you can seamlessly incorporate them within the measure.

Some Nights (page 182)

"Some Nights" (2012) is a song by the indie-rock band fun. that pits lyrics that speak of loneliness against a bright Afrobeat feel. The single peaked at #3 on the *Billboard* Hot 100 and was a global hit as well, going to #1 in Australia, New Zealand, and Israel. It has translated well to a variety of settings, having been heard in everything from television shows like *Harry's Law* and *Secret Millionaire* to a Southwest Airlines commercial. The song's glorious vocal harmonies are captured in piano chords in our fun and handy arrangement.

Played in the easy key of C major, "Some Nights" is built from just three chords: C, F, and G. To help distinguish the different sections, this arrangement uses a variety of strategies. The song kicks off with an approach that incorporates root-fifth sonorities in the left hand and blocked chords in the right hand, with a minimum of rhythmic independence between the parts. Later, the prevailing texture involves the vocal melody played in the right hand, supported by the occasional chord, and a single-note syncopated bass line operating in an independent rhythm. Textural changes like these keep things interesting.

Someone Like You (page 192)

Another powerful ballad by Adele, "Someone Like You" is the English singer-songwriter's signature number. A pop ballad inspired by a relationship that went sour, the single became an international #1 hit, topping the charts in countries from Australia to the United States. The original recording features voice and piano; solo instrumentalists will appreciate that the piano part in our arrangement matches the original recording note-for-note in some places, but also incorporates the vocal melody in the right hand.

"Someone Like You" has an interesting push-and-pull happening between the vocals and the piano chords. During the verse, for example, the spare, wistful vocal melody sticks to a lower range while the chords move slowly, at the rate of one per measure. Then at the prechorus, the vocal phrases are more rhythmically active, with streams of 16th notes, while the chord progression moves faster, at the rate of two chords per bar. Next, at the chorus, which starts with the lyric "Never mind, I'll find…," the vocals seem almost defiant as they leap to a higher register while the chords remain more active. Be sure to exploit these differences with dynamics, and by holding back at first, then playing more assertively in the chorus.

Somewhere Only We Know (page 200)

Formed in 1997, the English alternative rock band Keane toiled for years before they achieved great success with the single "Somewhere Only We Know," from their debut album, *Hopes and Fears* (2004). The group's first best-selling single "Somewhere Only We Know" peaked at #3 on the UK Singles chart and #11 on *Billboard*'s Adult Top 40. This arrangement nicely distills the bright pop sound of the original recording.

"Somewhere Only We Know," in the key of A major, is for the most part a very straightforward song. But do scan ahead for any areas that might trip you up. For instance, in certain spots the left-hand part switches between the bass and treble clefs. And although the song is almost purely *diatonic* (falling within the key of A), some isolated accidentals seem to leap out of nowhere. Keep the full chords less prominent than the melody, and be gentle with the repeated notes to create a beautiful lyrical mood while keeping the tempo moving.

Speechless (page 167)

Better known as Lady Gaga, the modern diva Stefani Joanne Angelina Germanotta is the Millennial Generation's biggest superstar, known as much for her audacious sartorial style as for her bold pop songs. From Lady Gaga's third EP, *The Fame Monster* (2009), "Speechless" was written for her father, to convince him to undergo the open-heart surgery that he'd long needed to repair a defective valve. (Her appeal was successful.) This power ballad, which betrays the influence of David Bowie and Queen, peaked at #1 on *Billboard*'s Hot Singles chart. It works quite well as a piano-vocal-guitar arrangement.

"Speechless" was recorded in the key of D♭ major, but for your convenience we've arranged "Speechless" in the more user-friendly key of C. The song has a nice infusion of *chromatic* notes, those falling outside of the key. For instance, the E♭ in the piano part of the first measure is an example of a *blue note*, or a flatted third in a major key. The F♯s in the first and second bars are chromatic *lower neighbors* to the surrounding Gs. At the end of the third bar, there's a chromatic *passing chord*, F♯, which connects two diatonic chords, F and Gsus. When strategically deployed, alterations like these can add soul to a song.

Stay (page 206)

Recorded by the Barbadian singer Rihanna for her seventh album, *Unapologetic* (2012), "Stay" is a pop ballad featuring the guest vocalist Mikky Ekko, a Nashville artist who also wrote the song. "Stay" earned the ever-prolific Rihanna her 27th million-selling single and her 24th Top 10 on *Billboard*'s Hot 100, breaking Whitney Houston's record of 23. With its plaintive melody and vulnerable lyrics, the song has been covered by everyone from the *American Idol*-winning singer Adam Lambert to the Jonas Brothers.

"Stay" shouldn't present any great difficulties on the piano. The ultimate goal of the song is to play it with expression. In order to do so, first get acquainted with the lyrics and the emotions they conjure up, and keep all this in mind when playing the piano part. Remember, this song is passionate. Also, although the notation has just one dynamic marking, *mp* (*mezzo-piano*, or moderately quiet), feel free to play with varied dynamics throughout the song. For example, you could build in volume and intensity as you approach the chorus section and back off in the verses.

Sunday Morning *(page 212)*

Not to be confused with the Velvet Underground, Earth, Wind & Fire, or No Doubt songs of the same name, "Sunday Morning" was a big hit for the pop-soul band Maroon 5 back in 2004. The fourth single from the group's debut album, *Songs About Jane*, "Sunday Morning" peaked at #4 on *Billboard*'s Adult Pop Songs chart and was a worldwide success as well, traveling all the way to #1 on the Belgian chart. The tune appeared on the soundtracks for *Something's Gotta Give* and *Love Actually* and also as downloadable content on *Lips*, the Xbox 360 game.

If "Sunday Morning" sounds jazzy to you, there's good reason: It's based on the most common chord progression: ii–V–I (Dm–G–C in the key of C). In fact, the song is one big C major ii–V–I progression, so after you learn the four-bar introduction, then you'll basically know the entire song. Note that there are some subtle harmonic variations throughout. For instance, the Cmaj7 chord (C–E–G–B) sometimes includes the ninth, D, making it a Cmaj9 chord; similarly the G7 chord (G–B–D–F) sometimes adds the 13th degree, E. Study the differences in sound between these sonorities, and try borrowing some of the chords for use in your own music.

A Thousand Years *(page 224)*

Another moving number by Christina Perri, "A Thousand Years" was recorded for *The Twilight Saga: Breaking Dawn Part 1*. Being included on this soundtrack was a dream achieved for Perri, a devoted fan. The song is inspired by the love affair between the characters Edward and Bella throughout the saga. Released as a digital download worldwide in 2011, this piano and acoustic guitar-driven ballad has sold over two million digital downloads and peaked on *Billboard*'s Adult Pop Songs chart at #7. Whether you play the piano or the guitar, our arrangement will let you take a stab at this lovely ballad.

"A Thousand Years" is in 3/4 or waltz time, that is, three quarter notes per bar. And it is felt in 1, which is to say you should count by tapping your foot only on the first beat of each measure. When you play through the song, especially the introduction, with its tied long notes, avoid the temptation to rush the tempo. If necessary, use a metronome, first clicking on all three beats, and then just the first beat. Throughout, add slight emphasis to beat 1 and strive for a lilting feel, because a waltz is a type of dance music.

Too Close *(page 232)*

"Too Close," a tune by the British singer-songwriter Alex Clare, was released as a single in the United Kingdom in April 2011 but didn't achieve international success until a year later, after it made an appearance in an advertisement for Microsoft's Internet Explorer 9. The song then sold over two million downloads in the U.S., reached #7 on *Billboard*'s Hot 100 and appeared during player entrances for a number of Major League Baseball teams. With this exposure, Clare, who had previously been dropped from his record label, saw his musical fortunes turn around. As with, "I Knew You Were Trouble.," our arrangement of "Too Close" approximates this song's dubstep influence on the piano.

A good performance of "Too Close" requires the rhythms to be played crisply and precisely. Be sure to really zero in on the rhythm of the bass clef in bar 9 and bar 17, because these patterns are what propel the song. Don't be discouraged if you need to take out a metronome, slow things down, and subdivide in order to nail these parts. In the chorus, quarter-note triplets make an entrance in the left-hand part. If you need to remember how to count these, refer to the notes for "Just Give Me a Reason." One more thing: In the treble clef at the bottom of the second page of music you'll see tremolo markings on the chords. Here, rapidly alternate between the notes using wrist action, and be careful not to let the chords ring beyond their designated values.

Wanted *(page 238)*

The young singer-songwriter Hunter Hayes wrote "Wanted" (2012) as a means of conveying how a great relationship could be transformed into something even better. This catchy love song charted impressively, peaking at #1 on the U.S. Country charts and at #16 on *Billboard's* Hot 100. In 2013 it was nominated for a Grammy Award for Best Country Solo Performance, solidifying Hayes' status as one of country music's brightest stars.

Although it starts off on an Fsus2 chord, "Wanted" is in the key of C major. In the accompaniment, the song makes great use of different types of suspended chords. An Fsus2, for instance, is an F triad (F–A–C), in which the third degree, A, has been replaced by the second, G. Likewise, a Csus2 chord is a C triad (C–E–G) with its second, D, replacing the E. The song also uses suspended fourth chords, labeled simply as "sus," in which the third is replaced by the fourth. For instance, a Csus chord is spelled C–F–G. To best appreciate how these chords sound and function, play each sus chord, then its major-chord counterpart. You'll hear that the sus chords create a rich, ambiguous sound that calls for resolution.

When I Was Your Man *(page 219)*

Bruno Mars was only four years old when he began his musical career by fronting his uncle's band in Honolulu, Hawaii. Two decades later, Mars is a highly successful singer-songwriter and producer who often writes in a modern R&B style. One of Mars' greatest hits is his piano-driven breakup ballad "When I Was Your Man," which was inspired by real-life heartbreak. The song was a smash hit around the world, reaching #1 on the U.S. charts and hitting the Top 10 in countries from the Czech Republic to Scotland. Here you'll find everything you need in order to play and sing this vulnerable number.

"When I Was Your Man" should be played with a 16th-note swing feel. If you need to be reminded what that's all about, read the performance notes to "Bad Day." It might seem as though the bass part gets complicated in spots, but if you inspect it closely you'll see that it's actually pretty simple. The left hand sticks to the root of each chord, often played in octaves and with just a little syncopation thrown in here and there. Instead of learning the bass part note-for-note, try improvising it. Just look at the guitar chord frames for the name of each root note, play in octaves or in single notes or a mixture, and throw in rhythmic embellishments as you see fit.

You're Beautiful *(page 244)*

The former British army officer and singer-songwriter James Blunt ascended to fame with his 2005 debut, *Back to Bedlam*. From that album, "You're Beautiful" is a song inspired by an encounter on the subway in which Blunt saw an ex-girlfriend with a new beau. The song is Blunt's most successful single to date, having reached #1 in ten countries around the world, including the UK, the U.S., and Spain. This beautiful ballad is perfectly suited to a piano arrangement.

"You're Beautiful" is played in the jazz-friendly key of E♭ major. And although this fact might not be obvious, there are some jazzy things going on in the melody. In the verse, Blunt makes the most of just three notes, G, B♭, and E♭, milking them with syncopations in the way a skilled improviser might explore a motif. A liberal amount of rests are found, giving the music the space to breathe. To put it another way, less is often more, something to consider in your own composing.

Love Song

Words and Music by Sara Bareilles

My Immortal

Words and Music by Ben Moody, Amy Lee and David Hodges

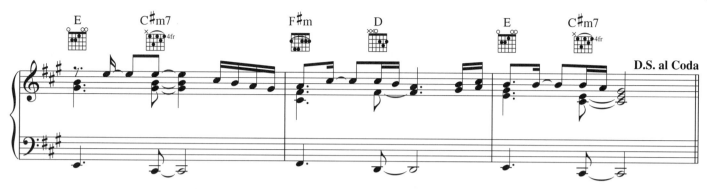

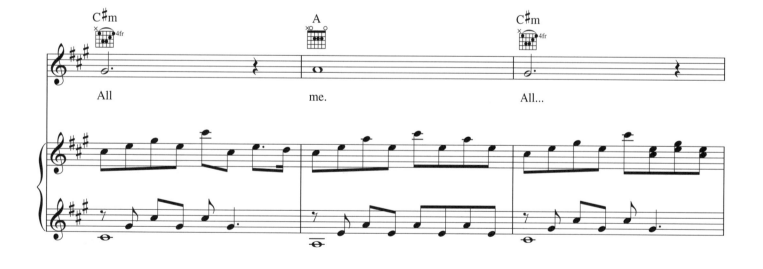

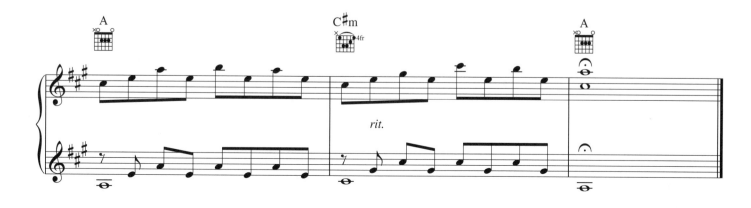

The Luckiest

Words and Music by Ben Folds

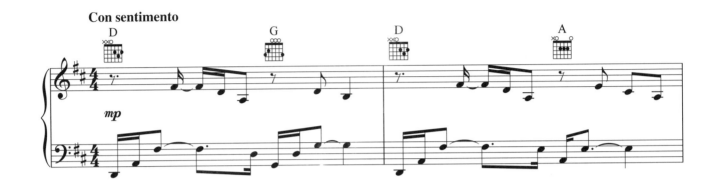

Lyrics:
I don't get man-y things ___ right ___ the first ___ time. ___ In
I'd been born fif - ty years ___ be - fore ___ you in ___ a house ___
door there's an old ___ man who lived in - to his nine - ties and ___ one day ___

Next to Me

Words and Music by Emeli Sandé, Harry Craze, Hugo Chegwin and Anup Paul

Pyramid Song

Words and Music by Thomas Yorke, Jonathan Greenwood,
Colin Greenwood, Edward O'Brien and Philip Selway

The Scientist

Words and Music by Guy Berryman, Jon Buckland, Will Champion and Chris Martin

I'm go-ing back to the start.

Speechless

Words and Music by Stefani Germanotta

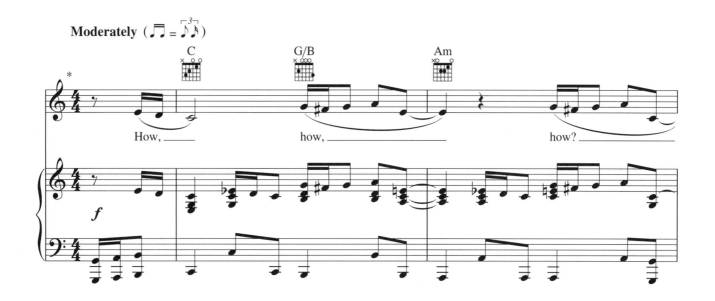

How, _____ how, _____ how? _____

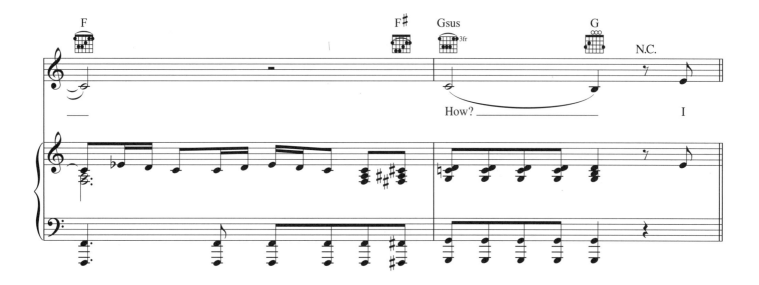

How? _____ I

can't be - lieve _ what you said to me, _ last night we were a - lone. _____ You threw your

Recorded a half step higher.

Skyfall

from the Motion Picture SKYFALL
Words and Music by Adele Adkins and Paul Epworth

Some Nights

Words and Music by Jeff Bhasker, Andrew Dost, Jack Antonoff and Nate Ruess

Moderately, with a March feel

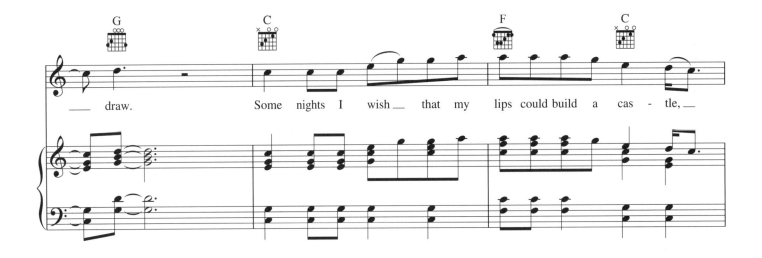

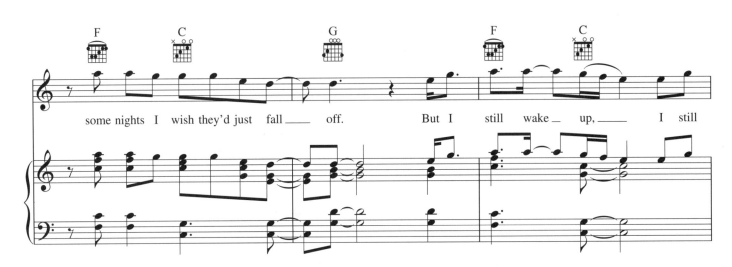

Someone Like You

Words and Music by Adele Adkins and Dan Wilson

Somewhere Only We Know

Words and Music by Tim Rice-Oxley, Richard Hughes and Tom Chaplin

some-where on - ly we know? _____ Some - where on - ly we _____ know. _____

So why don't we _____ go, so why don't we _____ go? _____

Ah. _____

Stay

Words and Music by Mikky Ekko and Justin Parker

Moderate Ballad

Sunday Morning

Words and Music by Adam Levine and Jesse Carmichael

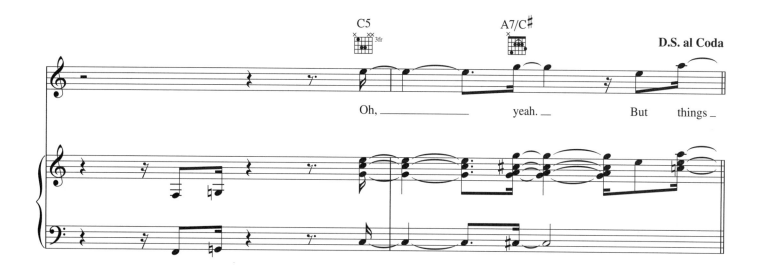

Oh, _____ yeah. __ But things _

- ing. Driv in' slow, _____ yeah, __ yeah. _____ Ahh, yeah, _ yeah. _____ Ahh, all _

When I Was Your Man

Words and Music by Bruno Mars, Ari Levine, Philip Lawrence and Andrew Wyatt

A Thousand Years

from the Summit Entertainment film THE TWILIGHT SAGA: BREAKING DAWN - PART 1
Words and Music by David Hodges and Christina Perri

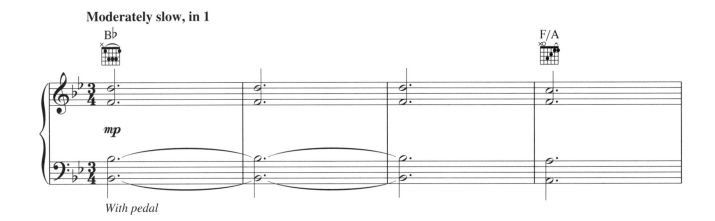

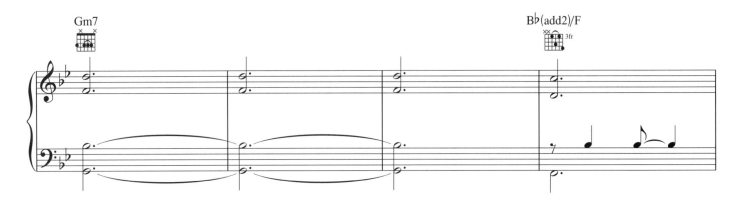

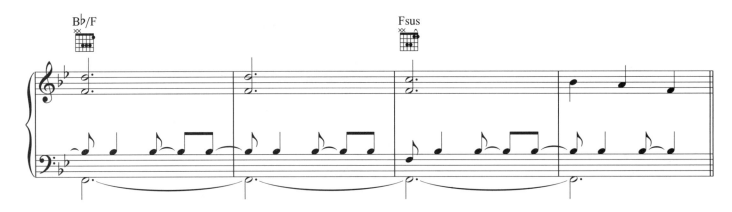

Too Close

Words and Music by Alex Claire and Jim Duguid

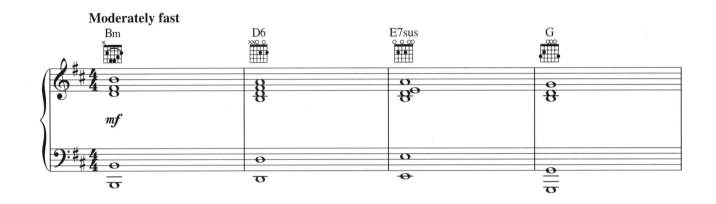

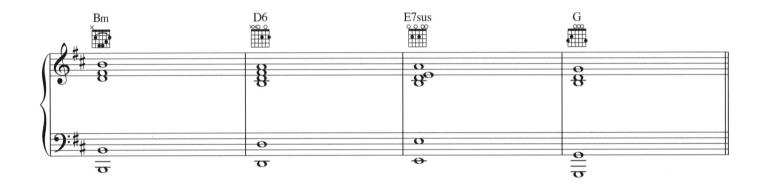

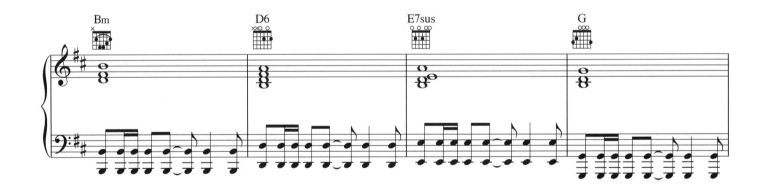

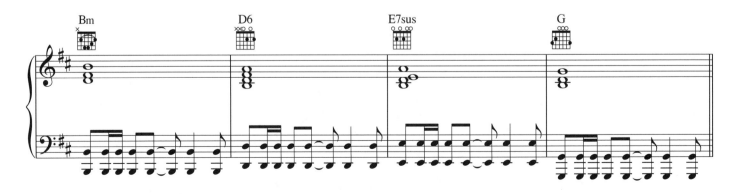

feels   like   I   am   just   too   close __ to   love ____ you. __

So   I'll   be   on   my   way. __

Wanted

Words and Music by Hunter Hayes and Troy Verges

You're Beautiful

Words and Music by James Blunt, Sacha Skarbek and Amanda Ghost

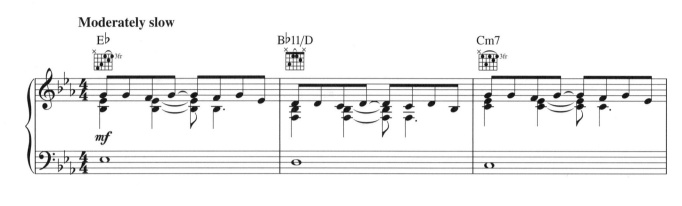

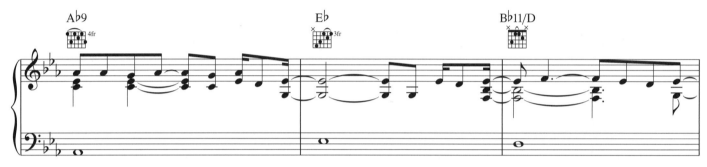

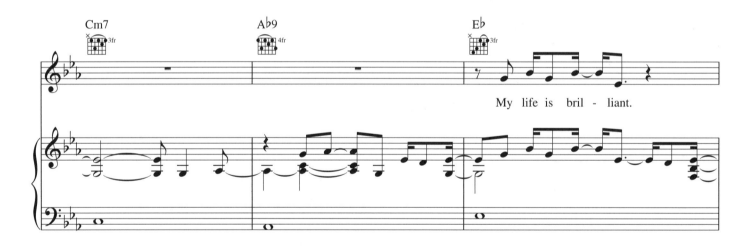

My life is bril - liant.

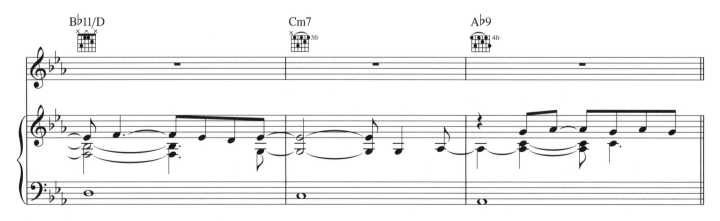